MOMMY, COME HOME

The 'New' Trend to Tradition: Bringing Up Your Own

By Sandra K. Gillmore
Home schooling mom of ten

TABLE OF CONTENTS

Preface

Come, sit down and have a cup of TEA (time of encouragement and affirmation.) I want to be your friend and help you through this dilemma in which you find yourself. You feel the tug of your little one's heart on your own and you want to at least consider the option of full-time-stay-at-home mothering, but with so many obstacles and opposing opinions blocking your field of vision, you can't see the facts clearly. Go ahead, sit down with your tea and put your feet up. You look stressed. Take a deep breath. There, that's better. Now, let me help you sort out your thoughts and separate fact from fiction; truth from fantasy. I am not here to bash you career moms or cast judgment to you single mothers, by whatever circumstance. (You, too, may benefit from some of my ideas and even find a way to stay home despite your extremely difficult circumstances.) I wrote this book specifically to encourage you - a loving mother- to consider options that may better equip you to provide for your own needs, your family's needs, and in turn, help the body of Christ, American society and ultimately the world, by more completely fulfilling your sacred and privileged role as *mother.*

What's this? Oh, I think this note is for you:

Dear Mommy,

Mommy, I know you by scent and by sound
I will sense the difference if you're not around
I ache to be rocked and nursed in your arms
It's upsetting to hear those wake-up alarms

Please don't rush around and ignore my loud cry
If you are leaving me, please tell me why

I don't mean to be trouble. I try to be good
I just need my Mama so I'll feel understood

Whatever is out there that calls you away
"God, make it stop!" I say when I pray
My Mommy's been trapped by a great big monster
If she's not saved quickly I'll think I have lost her

I don't see her face all the day long
Where has she gone? I fear something is wrong
My cries don't get answered – I just fall asleep
And dream of my Mama who cares when I weep

I know she must love me. I won't give up hope
By my cries at night she'll know I can't cope
Maybe she'll hear all the words of my heart
And may God show my Mom we just can't stay apart

I pray she'll be there to teach me new words
Someday we'll be outside just listening to birds
We won't be in a hurry to rush anywhere
We'll just build with blocks or rock in the chair

Maybe she'll finger-paint or color with me
I hope Daddy and she make a sibling for me
I'll listen and learn anything she teaches me
When I'm into mischief I'll pray her arm reaches me

I dream that someday my Mom will be there
To talk, laugh and cry, and deeply we'll share
The days will go fast, into weeks, months and years
I hope Mom will be there for my tears and fears

If I get the chance to know who you are
Then, Mom, I'll try hard to never stray far
But if you're not there during most of my life
I'm sorry we'll both face a mountain of strife

I love you, Mama, and if you love me
Please stay home for Daddy and me

Can a mother forget her infant,
be without tenderness for the child of her womb?
Even should she forget,
I will never forget you. (Isaiah 49:15)

Chapter 1: Why Stay Home?

We moms have become very concerned about school violence,
premarital sex at decreasingly younger ages, drug addiction, and
essentially the overall rebellion that is seemingly inescapable
regarding today's children - particularly teenagers. Is there a
solution? I believe there is. I believe it all begins in the home.
We've all heard that. But when we spend the great majority of our
lives *outside* the home, can anything really *start* at home? More
often than not, our homes have become a mere 'stopover' to rush
in and out with essential items, sleep, and, less often anymore, to
share a meal.

Do you really buy into the notion that you 'have to work?' *See
to it that no one captivate you with an empty, seductive philosophy
according to human tradition, according to the elemental powers
of the world and not according to Christ, (Colossians 2:8)*

In the following chapters I will try to encourage you with facts
and ideas that will give you confidence in knowing that you can
still meet your family's needs (financially) by staying at home, and
also satisfy so many more of their needs! You can build an
environment in your home conducive to molding your child's
character.

Your husband and child(ren) need you to be there for them -
emotionally, physically, and spiritually. Many a mom has
discovered that 'having it all' or even 'having it all but not all at
once' is really a downward spiral into the abyss of perpetual

busyness. How can we expect to build a stable and loving marriage and raise up respectful, morally-upright children when we are only home long enough to throw a quick meal on the table, shove a few loads of laundry through the machines, tend to our paperwork, and contemplate how tired we are? How can we meet the needs of our family when we ourselves are so rushed and exhausted all the time? Who told us we 'have to work?' None of us really believe that our children are getting 'quality time' when they are exhausted, hungry, overwhelmed with homework, and being rushed to and from day care and after-school activities, do we?

So, if you want an answer to 'Why should I stay home?,' it is to invest the time needed to build a peaceful, intimate environment that encourages open dialogue, prayer and relaxation, fun and recreation, outreach to the community, and *love*. You may have heard before that love is spelled T-I-M-E. There simply is no substitute for your *time*.

Biblically speaking, the women are to be to be, *"self-controlled, chaste, good **homemakers**, under the control of their husbands, so that the word of God may not be discredited." (Titus 2:5, emphasis added)*

Husbands are told to care for their families. *"love your wives, even as Christ loved the church and handed himself over for her" (Ephesians 5:25).* The mother's primary role is *nurturer*. Many husbands, including my own, are very nurturing and can fill-in and reinforce what we moms are instilling in our children all day every day. However, their minds are designed by God differently and fathers are not equipped to as easily sense a baby's need the way a mother can (especially if she's breastfeeding and has the advantage of God-given hormones to help her stay tuned-in to her baby.) We could brag all year about the wonderful qualities of countless husbands/fathers, but that's not reason enough to usurp God's authority and trade God-ordained roles within the home. Fathers were created to be the *provider* and *protector* of our families.

Husbands who choose to share household and childcare responsibilities with their working wives wind up exhausting themselves, inhibiting their career growth with absenteeism, arriving late, leaving early, and leaving in the middle of the workday to attempt to meet their family's needs. Raising children and caring for the home is, in reality, a full-time job. According to scripture, that job belongs to the *mother*.

It's true that Proverbs 31 provides evidence that in certain situations it is biblically acceptable for a mother to work (for income). But if you read closely, you'll see that the reference implies a home-based business which does not steal as much family time. This book of Proverbs also implies that the children's needs are fully met at the time the mother pursues any outside work. There is no reference made to suggest that someone else is caring for the mother's children for long periods of time on a regular basis. You can come to your own conclusions, but the way I see it, the only possibility of even coming close to being the

'Ideal Wife' described in Proverbs 31 is to work and minister from the home:

When one finds a worthy wife,
*   her value is far beyond pearls.*
Her husband, entrusting his heart to her,
*   has an unfailing prize.*
She brings him good, and not evil,
*   all the days of her life.*
She obtains wool and flax
*   and makes cloth with skillful hands.*
Like merchant ships,
*   she secures her provisions from afar.*
She rises while it is still night,
*   and distributes food to her household.*
She picks out a field to purchase;
*   out of her earning she plants a vineyard.*
She is girt about with strength,
*   and sturdy are her arms.*
She enjoys the success of her dealings;
*   at night her lamp is undimmed.*
She puts her hands to the distaff,
*   and her fingers ply the spindle.*
She reaches out her hands to the poor,
*   and extends her arms to the needy.*
She fears not the snow for her household;
*   all her charges are doubly clothed.*
She makes her own coverlets;
*   fine linen and purple are her clothing.*
Her husband is prominent at the city gates
*   as he sits with the elders of the land.*
She makes garments and sells them,
*   and stocks the merchants with belts.*
She is clothed with strength and dignity,
*   and she laughs at the days to come.*
She opens her mouth in wisdom,
*   and on her tongue is kindly counsel.*
She watches the conducts of her household,
*   and she eats not her food in idleness.*

Her children rise up and praise her;
her husband, too, extols her;
"Many are the women of proven worth,
but you have excelled them all."
Charm is deceptive and beauty fleeting;
the woman who fears the LORD is to be praised.
Give her a reward of her labors,
and let her works praise her at the city gates.
(Proverbs 31:10-31)

I would like to paraphrase the above scripture in practical terms to give you an idea of how a Mom in the twenty-first century could begin to live this out, practically speaking. Keep in mind, although I have used some examples from my own life, I don't dare to proclaim I am even close to living up to the 'Ideal Wife'. I am still on the journey, like us all. . .

The Ideal Wife of the 21st Century:

When a man finds a woman,
    willing to care for him with her whole life,
he has found a prize worth more
    than the largest winning lottery ticket.
Her husband, trusting that she will be home
    for him and their children,
has found a blessing to behold.
She tries to listen to him
    and look out for his health and spirit,
all the days of her life.
She shops the clearance racks
    at the local discount store,
and checks out garage sales and thrift shops
    to save money on clothes.
She searches the web for the best deals
    on special birthday and Christmas gifts.
She starts the breadmaker the night before,
    and keeps healthy ingredients on hand

12

to make hearty meals for the family.

She buys healthy foods
        according to the best prices,
careful not to overindulge in junk food.
The money not spent on convenience items
        is used toward short trips with the family
to nature parks and historic sites
        promoting education and appreciation
for God's creation.
She keeps in shape by walking
        or aerobic training,
in order to be ready
        for heavy cleaning jobs
and lugging toddlers on her hip.
She stays up late paying the bills,
        and figuring business orders
(if she has a home business.)
Sometimes she stays up late
        to get the home school papers graded
(if she is home-schooling.)
She opens her home to exchange students,
        foreign refugees, or a lonely mom.
She enjoys hosting prayer groups
        or Bible studies in the home,
  with her family (or with other women.)
She always plans ahead for tasks,
        anywhere from mending and replacing clothes,
to ordering new school books.
She may sew, crochet, or knit for her family,
        (unless she's untalented in that area like *me,*) or
she may write a song or a poem for her family,
        or plant a lovely flower garden.
Her husband, whether employed as
        a garbage collector or a brain surgeon,
never has to worry about the home
        or the children when he goes off to work.
His wife is watching over everything and everyone.

She is preparing snacks for the soccer team,
    and teaching a teen to drive.
She is driving a child to the doctor,
    and teaching the children
to resolve their differences.
She is making playdough,
    and allowing her children to be
creative with arts and crafts.

She is strong in the Lord,
    and feels joy from her children's progress.
She isn't overcome with anxiety about tomorrow.
She prays and plans for the future
    and leaves the rest in God's hands.
She *tries* to tame her tongue and speak wisely.
She checks on her children constantly,
  and sees to it that they are behaving
    in a godly manner.
She is readily available to her children,
    listens to them at any time they need her,
  and offers godly counsel for their ears.
She disciplines them as necessary
    throughout the day,
  and sticks to a household schedule
    that brings peace and order to the family.
She sets a good example by her self-control.
She doesn't eat ice-cream sundaes on the couch
    while watching late-night TV,
(well, okay, maybe only when she's VERY pregnant.)
Unless she is sick, you will find her busy
    keeping up with the laundry,
  and maintaining a running grocery list.
She takes delight in overseeing, and delegating
    the household chores to family members
so that each person feels valued,
    and contributes toward family harmony.
Her children speak to her in kind and encouraging words
    when she feels down or discouraged.

Her husband smiles and says "I love you,"
    and thanks her for all her hard work.
Sometimes she puts her foot in her mouth
    and says the wrong thing to friends at church.
She doesn't always fit in
    and her lifestyle is often misunderstood.
She sometimes gets weary of being asked,
    "Are you expecting again?"
when she's really just struggling
    to lose those previous-pregnancy pounds.
She loves the Lord and wants to do what is right.
She tries to remember that the reward
    is seen not in the world's eyes,
but in the eyes of her husband and children
    with Heaven as her ultimate reward.

Grandma is Surely the Next Best Thing. .

Maybe, but why should your children settle for second best? Grandma may have the best of intentions, by freeing you up so you can go live the "good life" she never had. Maybe Grandma didn't realize she *had* the good life all along (if she stayed home with you or your spouse as you grew up.)

In previous generations, families lived closer together, allowing grandparents the opportunity to become an integral part of their grandchildren's lives. They provided wisdom and insight, yet were unlikely to have physically cared for the children. This task is better left to a younger caregiver (ideally, the mother.) Today many families have become separated by distance from job transfers and military relocations. However, many families often arrange to live near grandparents for help with the children. Unfortunately, the sort of help sought after nowadays is often full-time childcare, which I believe to be totally inappropriate to the role of a grandparent.

When grandparents face the challenge of physically caring for their grandchildren, they may opt to embrace a more relaxed routine rather than sacrifice their own health and nerves. This may mean the child is not consistently disciplined and becomes 'spoiled.' The parents are then left with whiny, demanding, even disrespectful children who internally resent the lack of boundaries they so desperately need in order to learn self-discipline.

My own mother-in-law was convinced that if we give our child nothing else in this world, we should give him self-discipline, which is the essential ingredient needed in order to learn anything else. However, if we were to have recruited my dear mother-in-law as a full-time or even part-time caregiver for our children, her ideals would not have been fully realized. Through no fault of her own, age and health limitations would have prohibited her from physically and consistently acting on her convictions.

In an age-old childhood story, a family man goes to the wise man to complain about his house being too crowded. The wise

16

man replies that he should bring some chickens, cows, a horse and other animals into his house to teach him (step by step) 'how much worse' things could be. Finally, when the family man is at his wit's end, he runs back to the wise man one final time. The wise man, at this point, advises the family man to let all the animals out of the house and appreciate his family the way it is. The point of this story that I would like to bring to the table is that at no time was the wise man expected to *come* bring the animals into or out of the house. He stayed *right where he was,* and offered counsel and wisdom. Isn't this the role of a grandparent?

Naturally, grandparents love to hold their grandchildren and read to them or take them for short outings. They may even insist on giving us young parents a nice evening out from time to time as they welcome an occasional babysitting endeavor. Ultimately, the role of a grandparent, I believe, is to provide love and wisdom with an element of space. This ensures that they may also enjoy the fruits of their lifelong labors and participate in activities of their choice. In fact, many grandparents are just approaching a point in their lives in which they *can* embrace opportunities they may have missed while raising their own children. Even a healthy, younger grandparent is not wise to attempt to take over the parenting role, relieving the parents of their God-given responsibility.

Take, for example, this silly, yet realistic, outcome of repetitive generations of working mothers. One day a mother may ask her own mother or mother-in-law if she would assume the task of childcare provider for her grandchild. The grandmother may respond, "Well, gee, I've never really stayed home full-time and reared kids before, but I'll sure be glad to give it a try."

Think about this: How will *you* respond if your *own* children approach you about raising your grandchildren some day? Will you be eager for the job or feel cheated out of your 'golden years?' It all comes back to the old golden rule: Treat your parents the way you want to be treated when you are their age. *"Do to others whatever you would have them do to you. This is the law and the prophets." (Matthew 7:12)*

Let's focus on how much *more attentive* we could be to our aging parents and in-laws if we were not tied down with the constraints of employment. How often do you call your parents/in-laws? Do you enjoy emailing them? Just a short note about what little Jenny did this morning could be a real day brightener for a grandparent. When is the last time you had them over for dinner? Is the only time you get together in the context of them caring for your children? If so, a lot may be lacking in your relationship. For years we've enjoyed inviting grandparents to our Sunday family dinners. During the week the in-town grandparents have always been welcome to drop-in at any time for a short visit, or call to arrange a one-on-one outing with the 'grandchild of the week.' We have, at times, enjoyed vacations together, while at other times expressed our desire to be 'just us.' Whatever the case, I believe there should be mutual respect for privacy and schedule considerations while at the same time building an intergenerational bond to be passed down through the ages.

In cases of emergency (the mother dies or becomes physically or mentally unable to care for her children) a grandparent's full-time care would be a godsend, provided she is physically and mentally up to the task herself. However, more often than not, our grandparents are sweet-talked into taking on the role of their daughter or daughter-in-law by appealing to their ego ("You are so good with him, Mom, and this way we can save more money for his college education.") We've had some 'tough times,' (see that section later in this book) in which the grandparents were a godsend during illness, hospitalizations, and childbirth. It's hard for grandparents to feel like they can do much else during those times of need if they're already the full-time childcare providers for your children. What else *could* they do? On the flip side, we need to be available when our parents need *us* for doctor appointments or health and home maintenance concerns *they* may have.

Some offers are hard to refuse. New mothers are just forming their own opinions about raising their children. They may have their thoughts interrupted with such generous offers from their well-intentioned mother or mother-in-law that they just can't refuse. "Honey, we really struggled financially while raising you and your siblings on only one income. We want it to be different for *your* family so your children can have all the things you never

18

had. I'd be thrilled to care for little Johnny, and even another little one if that day should come. Just consider it our investment in our grandchildren. Dad will really enjoy having his little helper around all day too. Daycare is certainly no place for *our* grandbaby and it'll mean more money in the bank for you and your growing family."

After hearing that sort of loving, generous offer, it would surely be hard to turn it down! I have personally met Grandmas that are so dedicated they even homeschool their grandchildren.

It is true we should love and honor our parents, but not at the expense of our own parenting obligations. Remember that scripture passage from Titus? Here are the preceding verses that are advising the older ladies of the church. Just after giving advice to the older men, Paul writes this to Titus: *"Similarly, older women should be reverent in their behavior, not slanderers, not addicted to drink, teaching what is good, so that they may train younger women to love their husbands and children, to be self-controlled, chaste, good homemakers, under the control of their husbands, so that the word of God may not be discredited." (Titus 2:3-5)*

Now, if our generation of mothers was not taught these things, then we must find the truth on our own. We must act on our convictions, regardless of any well-intentioned pressure from our own parents, other relatives, or friends.

"In-Home Daycare Isn't So Bad"

If you have spoken with any moms who have chosen this option, you have likely heard the familiar heartache that the child becomes more attached to the daycare family than his own. This rings true with in-home nannies as well. It doesn't feel good to hear about all the 'firsts' from the loving person caring for your child ("You should have seen him take that first step today – it was precious!") when you know in your heart that you have missed a moment in time of your child's life that can *never be regained.* As I mention later in discussing home businesses, you can be sure that by your child being in the home of another mother for long periods of time, you are indirectly and unintentionally contributing to that family's stress. Those children may likely resent your child for intruding into their home each day. The mother watching your child, on the other hand, is indirectly enabling you to escape your duty as full-time mother.

"My Kids Would Drive Me Crazy!"

Have you ever considered the reason your children may drive you crazy may be that they do not share your value system? Can we really expect that they will know what our standards are if the great majority of their day is spent in school and daycare? It is only natural that children will emulate the values most encompassing their environment. By this same principle, children grow to more highly revere the values of their parents over any peers or other influences, once they have been immersed in the *consistency* of family life.

Are your children destructive? Do they seem to do *anything* to get your attention? How can a mother keep her little toddlers from scribbling on the wall or squishing the butter? This is one example where developmental needs must be met. Little children need to be permitted to be tactile. Make playdough. Let them color with washable markers, finger paint, paint with brushes, and be creative with beans, buttons, blocks and puzzles. If they are allowed to be creative on a regular basis with your supervision, they will have

20

little inclination to go sneaking through the house looking for mischief.

Many families have completely sectioned off portions of their homes for the children to play. I don't think this is wise. Children are not taught to organize their toys or care for them responsibly in this way. The play room becomes a dumping ground for broken toys. If children were properly trained in how to play, and where to put their toys, it would not embarrass us to have them play out in the main part of our home. If they are truly a treasured part of our family, it doesn't seem appropriate to banish them to the basement or an upstairs bedroom.

In addition, children are often left to decide for themselves how they will be entertained. In some homes, the TV and computer are completely free-reign to children of all ages. Even if all the programs are wholesome or educational, this permissiveness actually cripples our children's minds and squelches their creativity in a very hypnotic way.

They need a strong, steady influence from their loving mother to gently but firmly instill in them an understanding of good moral character. This can't be in a 'crash course,' but must be much like the old school of apprenticeship whereby we invest the time and repeat the lessons numerous times until it becomes 'second nature.'

Did our children *ask* to be brought into this world? Of course not. It was each of us and our husband who lovingly opened up our hearts and allowed God to work through us to create a new life in this world. It is, therefore, our responsibility to bring them up well-prepared to become productive citizens and committed Christians.

"It Won't Make a Difference"

You may feel so discouraged by the negative social environment in your child's school or even church groups that you think the few hours you would have at home with your child wouldn't have much impact. My personal conviction is that home schooling is a very effective option to consider. However, even with your child in public or private school, you can make a tremendous difference by *being there* for him.

My mother made the commitment to stay home as long as she felt she could. When I was fourteen, my father passed away after a very lengthy illness. The circumstances were that I usually came home from school to an empty house or a house with older teenage siblings who would often come and go on their own. Looking back, I believe my mother may have been enticed into thinking that joining the workforce at the time of my father's illness was the best thing for her mental well-being. She was extremely vulnerable and wasn't offered any counsel on alternative ways to survive such a traumatic situation.

Today as my mother looks back, she recalls feeling like an 'emotional disaster' during those years. My mother and I were very close, and fortunately the love and concern from my mother was so strong (from the years of foundation of her being home with us) that I had received enough moral grounding to prevent me from making even more mistakes than I already had. Possibly if my Mom were somehow able to be home even in those few hours after my school let out, it could have had a tremendous positive effect on my teenage years.

Thank God, most of us do not have the enormous burden of terminal illness in our immediate family. So, what is *our* excuse? We have to make a difference in society (within our careers, we think.) There are many ways outside of our careers to make a difference without sacrificing our children's moral upbringing, character building, and training. Think for a moment about your child's world. Most kids like to share about their day immediately after the activities occur. (Are we adults really any different in that regard?) The excitement or upset of the day's events will surely fade by the time you are able to listen to them. In fact, they may not be *willing* to share after waiting it out. How many times after asking about your child's day, have you been answered "fine" or "nothin'"? Kids will internalize feelings or put them 'on hold,' waiting for a loving person to understand them. Guess what happens when you aren't available? They will find a replacement for you. In my case, I found boyfriends. They seemed to 'understand me.' Other kids may turn to alcohol, drugs, gangs, and sex if they cannot relate to their peers. Even worse, some may turn to a potential child molester for wisdom and counsel.

Let's face it, Moms - we've got to be there for our kids! Do we really think we've 'succeeded' if our kids 'finish school, stay off drugs and don't get pregnant' before they are married? (And how would we know if our public-school daughter had an abortion, anyway, since in most states it is illegal for the school to tell us?)

As Christian mothers, in particular, we need to take seriously our God-given responsibility to:
"Train a boy in the way he should go;
even when he is old, he will not swerve from it. (Proverbs 22:6)
Please note, however, that this proverb is not a promise, but, rather, the proverbs are considered to be general principles. In other words, you can do your best and your child may still follow the wrong path, but that is unusual. The ones that do stray, usually come back to their roots.

Our children should be set apart from this world. If our children fit in with the crowd, we should be very concerned, and try to change that tendency! So, how *can* we make a difference? We can be there to do all the things that the Ideal Wife should be trying to do. We can ask our children about their daily life and give them wise counsel in dealing with the worldliness around them. Some of our children may become quite upset about the negative behavior that surrounds them. If it threatens to throw them into a depression, consider home schooling. This option would give them a protected environment to receive a firm foundation of their faith and morals before being 'thrown to the wolves,' so to speak. On the flip side, if your children seem enticed by the 'in-crowd' and desperately want to 'fit-in,' I hope you'll consider home schooling as an effective means to protect their little souls from corruption until they are firmly founded in their faith.

A Few Words About Home Schooling. . .

Home schooling is no longer some passing fad. It is here to stay. Consequently, there are countless books on the subject encompassing the reasons behind this educational and family-style choice, as well as many more books full of wisdom and experience on how to implement particular curriculum programs into your school at home. For this reason, I dare not even begin to offer you specific resources on this subject.

My suggestion for any interested moms is to use your favorite search engine on the web and type in 'home school.' It will stagger your mind. Next, type in your church's denomination before the words 'home school.' That will narrow it down a bit. Many Christian bookstores and even local discount and teacher supply stores have a multitude of resources and supplies as well. I will, however, provide *one* contact in the end notes for *Home School Legal Defense Association* (HSLDA). This organization will provide you with the legal requirements for your state, and, if you become a member, be available as your pre-paid legal service if ever you should need it.

Remember, that home schooling is not a 'cure-all' in and of itself. It doesn't guarantee a morally upright child anymore than attending church makes one a Christian. We must take full responsibility over the conduct, conversation, and code of dress (are they modest?) of our children. Even in the best of home school groups, some children emerge that are not being properly trained at home. So, let's not be fooled into thinking our children will be immune from negative influences in our local home school group. Although most of we Christian mothers realize that frequent prayer, church attendance and Bible study are important (if not essential) to instill uprightness in our children, some miss the other half of the job: being fully tuned in to our children to be sure they conduct themselves in a godly manner. I do believe, however, that the home school environment offers us moms the most flexible and *generous opportunity* to instill Christian character into our children.

Other Options for Education. . .

After the birth of our tenth child, and after home-schooling our children for ten years, we recently decided to enroll three of our oldest children into the public schools. The decision was a huge, nerve-racking change for all of us, yet we have been pleasantly surprised at how well the transition has gone. We are blessed with active student prayer clubs and wholesome extracurricular extensions in our school system. In another part of the country (we live in Middle Georgia) this could be a very different situation.

Our decision was based on the accumulative stress load of so much paperwork and teaching time coupled with so many little ones also needing lots of mommy time. We plan to continue home schooling our other children through at least middle school. We are now benefiting from a local church program which offers a parent's-morning-out, along with a short morning preschool program. Some home schoolers take advantage of programs like this to provide a break from interruptions during morning school time. Their toddler still spends the majority of the day at home and the older children can remain home schooled with less chaos. Other families have made use of home school video curriculums or satellite programs that meet their needs and offer some teacher's relief. Another whole world of choices is available through private Christian schools. Countless options are out there for educational choices, and, if we pray, discern and re-evaluate through the years, we can find the plan that works best for our family. *Finally, ... we earnestly ask and exhort you in the Lord Jesus that, as you received from us how you should conduct yourselves to please God--and as you are conducting yourselves--you do so even more. (1 Thes 4:1)*

I'll be Bored!

This is, in fact, a very valid argument. I, for one, would be *extremely* bored if I had only one or two kids and they were away at school most the day! Now, some of us may have only been blessed with one or two children, or not feel led to home school them. In these cases seek out plenty of opportunities to be creative within the home. It's not just 'busywork' if we are really seeking the Lord's will for our family.

Here are a few questions to think over: Are you opening your home to church groups or other families with children? Are your children welcome to invite friends over (provided they agree to abide by your house rules?) Do you involve the children in preparing meals? Do you teach your children how to manage the home or do you do everything *for* them? Do you take excursions with your children, whether pre-school age or older to educational outlets? (Even a trip to the grocery store *with* your children can be educational for them if they are allowed to *participate*.)

When is the last time you had a lemonade stand with your children? When we first tried this, the kids' number one customers were runaway criminals! The two men were stopping by in order to evade the cops who were after them. Imagine our shock when the police suddenly roared up our driveway, told me to take the kids in, and then pointed a gun at the 'customers.' They forced those bad guys to lie down in our yard, handcuffed them, searched them, and took them away – explaining that they were fugitives wanted in five states! In all the excitement, however, the officers became very thirsty and bought all the lemonade! The point is that I was there to experience this with the kids, and also to protect them from becoming too friendly with potentially dangerous strangers. Had I allowed them to conduct a lemonade stand while I was away 'at work,' the story certainly would have had a much grimmer ending.

Maybe you need more children to challenge you! Are you open to more blessings of life from the Lord? Are you open to adopting or foster parenting? Have you considered hosting an exchange student? We hosted two Japanese girls each during a different year, and it greatly enriched our children's cultural exposure. Opening our home to strangers was completely out of our comfort zone at first – but thank goodness we didn't let that stop us or we would have missed a huge part of God's plan for our family.

Since the Lord blessed us with a large, yet simple, home before He blessed us with all of our children, we've tried to use it for others as much as possible. At one point, a new friend was waiting on her husband to receive out-of-town career training and it was awkward to find a short-term rental situation. Being legally blind, it was not possible for the woman to easily meet the needs of her growing family with her husband absent. We offered our extra space to their family of five for a period of months. Our then same-size family was extremely blessed with my new friend's delicious talent for culinary arts and fellowship of each other, leading to life-long friendships.

At one point we offered free room and board for several months to two young pro-life law students. It was so much more enjoyable and rewarding than sending a check off to another charitable organization, hoping it would meet the needs we intended. We also offered portions of our home for low-income college students or troubled, depressed and mentally-ill individuals. At the time, we sometimes felt more 'stressed' than 'blessed' but we know God used us and our home to help these people in their time of need. The best part was that our children were involved in all of those experiences. Have you looked into hosting refugees? We hosted a Bosnian Family of three for several months, actually during the same period we hosted one of the exchange students. Incredibly, the exchange student had explicitly stated on her application that she loved children and wanted to help the poor! It was a crazy and blessed year since I was expecting our seventh child. This seemingly ridiculous situation must have been orchestrated by God because it wasn't possible for us to have planned everything out so creatively – we simply 'aren't that smart' as my husband often quotes, referring to that year. Due to the unique arrangement, our house guests had built-in opportunities to reciprocate for us by cooking or helping with our baby. The Bosnian mother, in particular, had thoroughly spoiled our (then) youngest child by the time they had moved out on their own. Because the language barrier was so intense, she was able to communicate by bonding with our little Robby and showing her appreciation by the things she did for us around the house (such as folding laundry.)

Unexpectedly, our church blessed us with a colossal basket of food that particular Thanksgiving. Other families dropped off clothing or offered much-needed errand-running for the Bosnian gentleman (who needed to make trips to fill out necessary forms for a green card application.) I was involved in helping the man obtain employment, which was quite a challenge considering his broken English. My husband, Dave, and our older children and I took turns teaching English to the Bosnian couple as well as to our exchange student, who was much better at reading and writing English than at *speaking* it. To this day both the Japanese girls and the Bosnian family keep in touch with us and continue to express appreciation for those months they spent in our home. No experience outside the home can compare to the intimacy of welcoming the displaced or needy into your family's abode.

Have you considered home ministry? We operated a Christian Coffeehouse in our home with contemporary Christian music bands for one weekend every month for four years. It was a great experience as far as exposure to a variety of music styles, as well as to folks from a variety of Christian denominations. The children were fully involved in preparing the home and refreshments each month. Once we were blessed with the opportunity to provide food and lodging to a traveling performer and his large family.

Although our home wasn't handicap-accessible, my husband frequently worked around that to piggy back a young paraplegic into our home to enjoy the coffeehouse music. We had met him through our involvement in another ministry outreach – a Christian performing arts group that ministered to nursing homes, juvenile delinquent centers and other places. This lonely young man was trapped inside the nursing home with no interaction or visits from anyone. We visited him frequently and discovered he was a gifted musician and songwriter. Later, with our guidance, he was able to become nearly fully independent and self-supportive in his own private apartment. Without investing the time to reach out, our family would have never been blessed by this man's courage and friendship. Preaching to our children about charity is *one thing*; involving them in it through their own home is *quite another*. It is so true that 'actions speak louder than words.'

Consider hosting a Bible study or family prayer group in your home. Not only are you reaching out spiritually, but you are training your children to do the same, and enriching your family relationships in the process. For an extended period we hosted a weekly Family Hour prayer group in our home. We never knew who was going to show up, but it was a time we spent praising the Lord in song and prayer. It's an extra opportunity for the children to invite friends from other activities and, again, keeps the family as the base.

We like to stay involved in our church's activities, but we limit ourselves so we aren't running to extra meetings on weeknights more than necessary. With a large family, in particular, we feel it's important to focus our activities as a family, choosing outreaches that can be held in the home, or that we can participate in together. However, each of our children also are allowed to be involved in at least one individual activity (ie: children's choir, soccer, track and field, guitar, gymnastics, art or dance lessons, political campaigning, drama, ceramics class, etc.) because we don't want them to get 'lost in the crowd'. Most of these opportunities I've mentioned would be impossible to facilitate in a family where the mom is working outside the home. Okay, I hope I've convinced you that 'being bored' is not a viable excuse to resist full-time, stay-at-home motherhood.

I'll be Lonely. . .

This, too, is a realistic, potential problem. Let's face it. Stay-at-home moms today are few and far between. We're oddballs. That's okay. To a certain extent, just accept it as the price we pay for obtaining (and maintaining) peace in our family. Pretend to be reading a book one day while your child's soccer practice is finishing up (or some similar situation) and open your ears to the woes of working moms. (Never enough time, always in a hurry, kids won't behave, etc, etc.) I'm not encouraging eaves dropping on others' very personal conversations -- just the little comments of frustration mothers often make to one another. Listen, with a prayerful, concerned heart and know that you are doing the right thing by being there for *your* family. Pray for other moms to get the courage to stay home as well. Then, start a group!

I've made the best friends of my life by starting prayer groups, and Bible studies. Try reaching out with an ad in your church bulletin or other source to attract like-minded mothers. If you aren't a 'starter,' then join a pre-existing group. I used to belong to Mothers of Preschoolers (MOPS), La Leche League (LLL), a breastfeeding support group, and others. The investment of these friendships will help give you the support you need, but be careful to balance these relationships with your most important ones: God and your family.

I remember enjoying some good friendships when our children were very young. Sometimes I would be on the phone for over an hour with another mom. She would scrub her dishes while she talked to me and I would scrub my floor with a baby in the baby carrier or nurse the baby and fold laundry. I am a regular chiropractic patient to this day partly, I'm sure, due to my crazy posture habits and crook-necked phone conversations of my youth! Our husband and children should be our primary relationships. As our children get older we will naturally have more time to invest in additional personal friendships of our own.

I Must Work For Financial Reasons

Are you a physician? An engineer? If you have a degree and make a sizeable income, you may be fooling yourself into thinking your career is your *vocation*. That may have bore truth before you conceived your first child, but once you are a mother, motherhood is your primary calling, secondary only to being a wife, and it goes without saying your relationship to God comes first.

Have you ever sat down and added up what you spend on daycare, professional attire, gas to and from work and daycare/school, dining out, fast-food and deli-food in, and other convenience foods? These can add up in a hurry. Have you considered what tax bracket you would be in if your household were on one income? Have you thought about the kind of car you drive and the reason you have it (need a newer vehicle for better gas mileage to and from work and to look more professional?) Did you buy a home based on two incomes? Do you breastfeed? Formula is expensive. Have you considered a diaper service or laundering your own cloth diapers? Do you cut your children's hair? There are videos to teach you how. Do you work-out in a gym? There are many free ways to exercise. Did someone tell you that you are morally obligated to pay for your child's college education? This could cripple your children into thinking the 'world owes them a livin'.

We have a personal friend whose family added up all the numbers and realized they were actually *losing* money by the mother working outside the home because of the similar expenses I mentioned above. Their family is not a unique case. But it takes courage to crunch those numbers and see where the money is really going.

What I'm getting to here is *lifestyle*. My husband and I started out quite well-to-do financially, and have gradually altered our lifestyle with each child to allow my presence in the home all these years. It hasn't been easy, but it has been well-worth the effort. Despite our trials and tribulations, our teenagers are the joy of our lives. We have a very close family relationship with each other and deeply treasure our time together.

31

Chapter 3:   What About Home Business?

Any Mom considering home schooling, in my opinion, should back away from home business ventures as a general rule of thumb. In reality, a home school *is* a business – albeit a non-profit one in IRS terms, but an *eternally* profitable one in God's terms.

I would like to share some words of caution here. Many of us have tried to be 'super-moms,' thinking we can easily succeed at a home business and still have ample time to invest in our home, husband, and children's upbringing, only to fall short and kick ourselves for being a 'failure.'

I operated a nutrition-and-cleaner-based business in our home for five years. I began the business shortly after becoming pregnant with our fifth child. The ages of our other children at that time were six, four, three, and one year old. Somewhere in that first year or so we also decided to begin home schooling. I was highly motivated to succeed in this health-based business due to the fact that our children at that time seemed chronically ill.

Every germ passing through the neighborhood always seemed to stop at our house and stay, as if we had a *'Welcome All Germs'* sign in our front yard! Therefore I wanted to use the products for the sake of our children's health and help my friends do the same.

The schoolwork for the children became increasingly complex as we added additional children (our own) to our classroom. Although my business was a great blessing to our health and I was able to help many families to become healthier through its products, I was foolishly setting my family up for a great deal of stress over the next few years.

It was during that same period of time we were also hosting one of our Japanese exchange students for the year, operating our monthly coffeehouse concerts, and had a series of needy renters living in the basement or upstairs portion of our home. Let's just say it got to be *too much*. As my husband says, "There are some folks who are committed, some who are overcommitted and some who **should** be committed!" As you can guess, we were in the third category at this point. I was fighting the myth you hear about, "just what **do** you do all day if you stay home, *anyway*?" I was out to prove to the world that I wasn't 'just' a stay-at-home-mom. Though I did feel called by the Lord to help people in many different ways, I had trouble sorting out who and when I should help, so I just figured if I said 'yes' to everything, all my bases would be covered!

My husband was *too* supportive of me. I wish he would have bossed me around a little and told me things needed to change. I was, in fact, pretty determined to use my exuberant energy for the 'good of the world,' and he figured there was no use in trying to slow me down. However, my husband, Dave, has always held very firm to his convictions that I stay in the home and we continue to home school.

Some nights I would be out the door to give yet another nutritional or cleaning demonstration or a ladies' facial party. I always tried to make sure the house was in order, the school work was done, and dinner was ready, so that Dave didn't have too much on his hands. However, I remember on days when something would go wrong and I just 'couldn't get it all together,' I would hand my poor husband some raw meat to cook or ask him to throw together a quick meal. Those kinds of days were taking place more frequently as time went on. . .

I knew that something needed to give. I couldn't bear the thought of putting the kids back in school. On the other hand, I very **loudly** suggested it to my husband many times because I couldn't see an easy way to back out of the business. I figured if I didn't have the responsibilities of home schooling, I could more easily manage the work load. Thank God, at those times, he never ceased to voice his authority in his quiet, loving tone. In those early years, under no circumstance would Dave ever consider putting his children back in the school system. (The older two had actually attended a private Christian school and we had fast grown weary of the friction caused with the schedules, extra school activities, fundraisers, etc, so we brought the children home.) He highly esteemed the worth of my presence in the home. Dave backed up his convictions with his own devotion of time – even teaching the children Math and Science every morning before going to work (his prime energy time) and grading their papers every night, *and has kept this up for the past ten years, I might add.*

So, it seemed, my only sane choice was to quit the business. I felt it would seem very 'unchristian' to close down our home ministry or close the doors to needy people. As God timed it, my husband accepted a job transfer to Georgia (we lived in Indiana at that time.) I felt this would be a great 'out' for my business to close. I could pass my customers over to the sweet woman who had mentored me for the previous five years.

At one point before our move, I was asked to speak for a couple of well-attended dinners and upheld as a 'super mom' who could home school five children and operate a very 'successful' business. One evening, while attending a similar dinner event, I was blessed to hear a speaker who was an extremely successful business woman and home schooling mom with a few children. Upon asking her some more detailed questions, in private, after her speech, she confided in me that she was not at all involved in her children's home education. She referred to herself as their 'principal' and wanted them in the home environment but used strictly video programs (albeit from an excellent, highly-rated curriculum program) to educate her children. Their work was graded by mail or email and her goal to keep the kids out of the public schools was accomplished. I felt the woman was very successful by her own standards, and by many others. However, I knew in my heart that what I wanted for *our* family was a much deeper relationship and more intense involvement in their education. Therefore, at that moment in time I knew I must find a way out of this business – and *fast!* We were moving soon. I sure wished God would give me a sign or speak to me...

Actually, God *had* been trying to speak to me for quite some time! Ever since I had started my business I seemed to have a perpetual case of laryngitis. There were days that I had to use amateur sign and body language to teach and discipline my children. It became embarrassing while on the phone trying to fill customer's orders and answer their questions about products. I found myself canceling my duties as a cantor and choir member at our church and was forced to opt out of solos for special services.

One Christmas Eve, although I couldn't speak an audible word, I was able to belt out, *Oh Holy Night* at the midnight Christmas service. It felt like an angel entered my body and sang for me! No one could believe it because they knew my voice was so hoarse. During our Christian coffeehouse (which we named *Heaven Bent Harmony,*) I rarely sang and was involved only in facilitating other bands, groups and soloists to minister with their talents. Looking back, I realize now that God was teaching me *humility*. He was showing me that He had the power to give and take away my talent, depending upon my motive for using it. He knew that my voice was essential in order to run my business and teach my children. Some would conclude that obviously I was just overusing my voice and that was all there was to it. I knew differently.

I actually visited several doctors and had tests run to be sure I had no tumors or permanent vocal chord damage. For several months I attended sessions with a speech therapist to learn how to use my voice without straining it. Singing became a thing of the past. I was a songwriter and had dreamed, along the way, of pursuing a part-time ministry or profession with that talent. I had even recorded an album in a studio with my best Christian songs all just before giving birth to our fifth child, Roch, and just before starting the home business.

We had made the decision to at least postpone having another child during my hectic business-building years. At times we even considered limiting our family to its (then) current size. However, my husband stood firm in his belief of natural family planning and never wanted to forsake that mystery-of-life potential, and I'm grateful for that. It always kept a special longing in our relationship and created mutual self-giving in place of self-gratification.

What made everything come clear to me was the time immediately following our move to Georgia. We were expecting our sixth child after a four year gap between children. At this time I was still feeling pressured by my upbeat business associates in Indiana. It was hard for me to be direct and tell them that after training and coaching me for five years I was going to *quit*. I remembered the scripture from my high school Christmas concert solo: *"Come to me, all you who labor and are burdened, and I will give you rest. Take my yoke upon you and learn from me, for I am meek and humble of heart; and you will find rest for yourselves. For my yoke is easy, and my burden light."* (Matthew 11:28-30) I truly asked God to 'show me a way out.' He did.

I went through all the procedures necessary to obtain a home occupation license. I have known several people, over the years, who avoid this hassle and claim their business is so small it 'doesn't count.' Well, unfortunately it *will count against them* someday if they are discovered avoiding local tax laws and home occupation restrictions. I knew I needed to set an honest example if I was intending to train others to follow in my footsteps as I had done in Indiana (the laws were more lenient there.)

When my turn to appear at the local city council home occupation meeting came up, I was asked by the presider if I held an inventory of product in my home. I stated that I certainly did, in fact $5,000 worth at that time. I believed the nature of the product I sold necessitated it being available at a moment's notice when customers weren't able to plan ahead for orders. In fact, our vacations had become less and less enjoyable due to the fact that so many customers rushed to fill their orders before we departed, and left countless messages on our answering machine for orders to be filled as soon as we returned! I also knew that these products were unique and needed to be personally demonstrated in order to pique the customer's interest in buying them. That also meant needing products on hand.

The presider firmly informed me that I would need to rent an office space in order to store the product out of the residential area. The reason for this was to avoid causing heavy traffic from customers in our neighborhood. I responded simply, "Thank you," and left. That was it! It was my way out! *Thank you, Lord.* Yes, many people told me then and now that I didn't really need that license anyway (after all it's just a city ordinance, right?) or I could have just had an exclusively on-line order business. But none of that mattered to me. God answered my prayer.

Since that time, I started another home business. This time our two older daughters helped me and I knew from the start it would be temporary. Believe it or not, I started the business while five months pregnant with our ninth child! I was thinking ahead to Christmas and getting rather depressed wondering how we would afford gifts for the children. Dave was long overdue for a raise and/or promotion and although he jumped at every opportunity, nothing led to its fruition.

I had an out-of-state friend with six children who also home schooled and seemed very happy and successful running a children's book business. I didn't even mention to her that I was thinking of signing-up under her (It's a multi-level-marketing company.) I simply announced to her that I had done so. No one lived in our area that could train me in the business, but I knew selling books would be much more straight-forward than cleaners and nutrition.

So my daughters and I bought our starter kit and off we went, showing countless moms these great books. I closed out our last party just before delivering the baby, only a few months later. We had accomplished my goal of accumulating $500 of excellent quality books for our children's Christmas gifts, along with some much needed cash.

I had undergone the trouble of regaining my business license with this endeavor even though it was a very short-lived business. It was in accordance with city ordinance since no inventory was necessary. In the meantime, I'm afraid I stirred up a little too much excitement for my upline due to my 'impressive' sales record so they were very disappointed when I suddenly quit.

As you can see, my second business venture was more in line with what our family could handle. In fact my family was quite involved with the business and it was easier to set aside to focus on the immediate needs of our family's newborn in the household.

So far, I haven't even addressed the issue of *income*. Some people have become very successful financially in their home businesses. In my experience, I found it hard to separate business from ministry. In fact, in my first business, I think I gave away so many vitamins and cleaners to help people, that I may have *lost* money! I had too large an inventory in order to please the customers, which greatly limited any cash that could have been used or invested for our family's needs. We also discovered that since our taxes were so complicated during those years, we had to spend quite a bit of money paying the accountant to figure it all out. So, some home businesses don't necessarily bring in the money a mom expects.

The book business I was involved with was a more practical set-up for a larger, busier family. The orders took place at the in-home book shows and were processed through the website. The books were then delivered directly to the customer from the company. This eliminated the need for home inventory plus a multitude of paperwork and packaging. From experience, I have come to the conclusion (along with the input and support of my husband) that looking for creative ways to save money is more cost-effective than running a business. It's easier to involve the children and takes far less time away from the family.

If you pursue a home business, count the cost. I would not recommend it to a home schooling family unless your children are older and you believe you are called to maintain (rather than expand) your current family size.

There are many home businesses that can involve your family. I have a sister whose family pursued a very successful clowning business (*The Funnybone Ticklers*) for years. They spent much time together rehearsing and performing, and even intertwined it with ministry outreach. Although it required hard work along with the fun, the clowning around created an ongoing opportunity for their family to learn cooperation and patience with one another. Their family unity is evident to this day.

On the other hand, I have another sister who operated a licensed in-home daycare for several years. She is extremely gifted with young children and wanted to avoid leaving the home for extra income. Looking back, she remembers how strained the family was during those years. She recalls that her home had to be extra clean to meet the strict standards, and her sons could not expect quality time from her when they might have most needed it – immediately after school hours. It was during those hours that many children were being picked up from their parents. Her business duties were certainly not on par with phone calls or product orders typical of other businesses, which could be set aside until after the children were in bed. No, when a two-year-old needs to potty – it's *NOW*. When a one-year-old is about to pick up a two-month-old infant – response time is *IMMEDIATE*. Although she made the best of a difficult situation, and seemingly helped many working parents in the process, she was not able to fully meet her own children's needs due to the enormity of attention required to operate a daycare facility. With the best of intentions, my sister was indirectly encouraging other mothers to leave their children for the workplace. After all, they were going to do it anyway, right?

In reality, none of us can ever *fully* meet our children's needs (nor should we.) But there are certain needs which can *only be met by us* – particularly we moms. In our hearts we know what those needs are and we know what it takes to fulfill them – *TIME.*

Hold on. There *is* a middle road somewhere in this dilemma. We don't need to work outside the home or conduct a home business in order to make ends meet. Neither do we have to avoid anything beyond clipping coupons and shopping garage sales in order to provide for our family within the constraints of a conservative budget. Why not be *creative*? Use your talents and skill to provide products or services to others on a case-by-case basis. This gives you the freedom to reject any offers that conflict with your family's most treasured spots on the calendar.

For example, I occasionally sing for weddings and funerals. In each case I have the freedom to decide if our family calendar can handle the commitment. Each job provides a little extra cash to complement my husband's hard-earned salary. My sister-in-law is extremely gifted in the art of calligraphy as well as painting. She has, from time to time, completed works of art or addressed wedding invitations for clients that are more than happy to pay for her services.

I have a friend who is extremely gifted in cake decorating. She has the option of charging for her services or offering them as gifts for special occasions (which also saves money.) Another friend of mine is a gifted and skilled photographer. She has utilized this talent creatively in order to accommodate her family's needs. Our son's guitar teacher chooses students based on his schedule limitations. For a mother, teaching a musical instrument or offering sewing classes could be a one-time series in the home to a group, or involve as little as one student. I taught piano lessons to a little girl next door for a couple of years. The lessons were in our home and always scheduled around the needs of our family. I also provided part-time childcare in our home for this sweet little girl and her sister for several years. They did not require nearly the intense care of toddlers as in the case of my sister's daycare business, and the playtime with our kids was a mutual bonus. One home schooling mom I know teaches youth drama workshops every summer at a local theater.

Granted, none of these ideas will bring in the cash flow of a full-time business in the home, but they do help, and spare the family from the stress that threatens to destroy the peace in our homes. If your husband isn't very supportive of pursuing other means to keep up with the bills, pray for him and ask God for a 'way out' – trust God. He'll find a way for you.

Chapter 4: Okay, I'll *Try* it.

When you started your first job, did you tell your boss, "Okay, I'll try it here for a week or so and see if I like it?" When you gave birth to your first child, did you proclaim, "We decided to give this parenthood thing a try and see what happens. If it doesn't work out too well, we can always trade him in for a puppy?" Of course not. Why would the decision to embrace full-time mothering be any different? I know many mothers opt for the 'stay home the first three crucial years' plan. I stated from my own experience the potential for teens to get into trouble due to lack of supervision in the home when they get off the bus. What about working when your children are in school, and getting home before they do? That's an option that may *work* for many families. But, what exactly are you looking for? Something that *works*? Something that *gets you by?* A schedule that is more *socially acceptable*? Or something **to grab hold of your family like the unshakably firm foundation you must have in order to thrive in spite of today's anti-family culture of death?**

How many couples divorced in *your* church last year? That's right. You probably know that the divorce rate for Christians is now the same or even higher than nonbelievers. *Participation in church activities is not synonymous with living out our faith.* In fact, I have seen some sad situations where a woman spends so much time at church that she neglects her own family! It's hard to believe, but it can and does happen, and none of us are immune to it.

Like marriage and career, families need a high level of commitment in order to reap the benefits we all want to see in our children's character. I strongly urge you, when making the decision to stay home for your family, to make it a permanent one. In my mind, this would mean until your youngest child graduates from high school or even college.   I know that sounds ridiculous to many of you, but just think back to your teen years. . . . .

41

It's Too Late for *My* Family

No way. It is *never too late!* All of us wish we could have done some things differently. But the past is in the past. We can only change the future. My husband and I both grew up in homes vastly different from the home we have created for our family today. Our parents created environments for us that were as loving and caring as they could possibly provide, profoundly more open and communicative than the households they grew up in. However, in looking back, we could see many 'holes' in our childhood family situations that we hoped to prevent in our new family.

At any point along the way, if you choose to put yourself back in the home as a full-time mother, you will reap abundant benefits. We have known many families, including ourselves, who have implemented improved parenting techniques or began homeschooling with older children. Some moms choose to breastfeed after having bottle-fed their previous children. Some start saving money later in life. In any case, these people all chose to improve some area of their life at some point. My father-in-law's personal motto is, 'When you're through changing, you're *through*.' It's so true. We all have so much to learn from each other.

This brings us back to *your* family, specifically your *children*. Who do you want them to learn from? Do you honestly believe that the local daycare providers and the local school system love your children the way *you* do? They may be the most loving people, but even in the best of cases, they can't and never should replace *you*. They are doing their job to care for your child. This means they are paid to try to keep your child physically safe, clean, well-fed and educated to the appropriate level.

Even in the most ideal situations (even private Christian schools,) your child's spiritual and emotional well-being is at stake. Learning about their faith is wonderful, but in order to internalize their belief system and express themselves from their heart, children need an intimate relationship with the people who love them the most – their parents.

What about those precious children in daycare and public school who are trying to sort out the conflicting value systems they have been exposed to for several hours each day? They question, "What is right and what is wrong?" Let me ask you a very personal question: Why *did* you choose to become a mother? If it was for the thrill of the 'experience,' that is wonderful – just remember the "experience" lasts a *lifetime*! Even when our youngest child grows up and goes out on his own, hopefully there will be a continuing relationship for the rest of our lives. It's a challenge for me to make it a whole week without talking to my *own* mother. She is a wealth of wisdom, love, encouragement and support to me. Maybe your relationship with your parents isn't something to brag about. That could be an even bigger motivator to be sure your children are more fortunate than you.

My beloved mother-in-law who passed away this year was orphaned at a very young age and rejected from relatives. She never felt like she totally belonged to a family. When she herself became a mother, she turned all this into something so beautiful. She never used her lack of being parented as an excuse for not being a good mother herself. For fifty full-time years, she poured herself into her marriage and family life. Her personal motto was, 'everyone gets twenty-four hours a day.' In other words, we all have freedom-of-choice as far as what we do with our time. She chose to spend it on her family. Regardless of what mistakes my dear mother-in-law may have made along the way, or what may have been misunderstood about her by other people, one thing was very clear: she sacrificed her life for her family.

She was a beautiful example of the immeasurable gift of time, of which there is no substitute. Expressing emotions wasn't easy for her, but she expressed herself through her cooking, baking, sewing, and just by *being there* for her family. My husband alone offered so much worry and grief to his mother with his childhood developmental difficulties, it's surprising she didn't just throw up her hands and march off into the workforce. Quite the contrary, she resolved that no matter what, she would do whatever was necessary to help her son, along with his two siblings, who had serious health challenges of their own. Looking back, it is miraculous that my husband pulled through to graduate from college, let alone be able to support a wife and ten children! His mom enjoyed having a career, too. But she had the patience to wait until her children had matured into young adulthood to re-enter the workforce. Her chosen jobs included involvement through family business ventures, thus extending her mothering opportunity even further. We all wish we could have started out with the level of commitment my mother-in-law had, so as to reap the benefits when the children become adults. But many of us stumble through those first years trying to make sense out of mothering and family life in the context of our very mixed-up modern society. That's okay. We've realized something doesn't fit here and we want to change.

No, it's never too late. No matter how you were raised, no matter how old your kids are, the day you choose to stay home with them will be a brand new start!

Chapter 5:   This Is Too *Counter-Culture*!

Bingo! That's it! Let's look around. Do we *really* want a family that fits into today's culture? Many families that have more than two children are 'blended families.' We all know the dreaded climbing statistics for single-parent families. How many families do you know where the parents are unmarried? Homosexual 'marriages' are becoming increasingly more acceptable. Many adoption agencies freely accept single women or men as adoptive parents. Who will raise *those* unfortunate children while their parent works all day? Yes, folks, these are the "families" of today. Do you want to 'fit-in?' Something tells you it's not right.

In a generation when homemaking is viewed as archaic, it takes courage to fulfill our role as a totally present mother shaping the conscience of our child's vulnerable mind. We *must* become counter-culture if we want our culture to change! As Christians we should actually be at *peace* in knowing we're not in the mainstream. Hebrews 11:13-16 tells us, *"All these died in faith. They did not receive what had been promised but saw it and*

44

greeted it from afar and acknowledged themselves to be strangers and aliens on earth, for those who speak thus show that they are seeking a homeland. If they had been thinking of the land from which they had come, they would have had opportunity to return. But now they desire a better homeland, a heavenly one. Therefore, God is not ashamed to be called their God, for he has prepared a city for them. " It sounds like we're being called to be **'Christ-culture!'**

We know Jesus highly esteemed women in the Bible, which was very counter-culture at that time. Matthew 26:6-13: *Now when Jesus was in Bethany in the house of Simon the leper, a woman came up to him with an alabaster jar of costly perfumed oil, and poured it on his head while he was reclining at table. When the disciples saw this, they were indignant and said, "Why this waste? It could have been sold for much, and the money given to the poor." Since Jesus knew this, he said to them, "Why do you make trouble for the woman? She has done a good thing for me. The poor you will always have with you; but you will not always have me. In pouring this perfumed oil upon my body, she did it to prepare me for burial. Amen, I say to you, wherever this gospel is proclaimed in the whole world, what she has done will be spoken of, in memory of her. "*

We know that Jesus loved little children and opened His heart to them at a time when children in adult situations were to be seen and not heard. This was also counter-culture.   Mark 10:13-16: *And people were bringing children to him that he might touch them, but the disciples rebuked them. When Jesus saw this he became indignant and said to them, "Let the children come to me; do not prevent them, for the kingdom of God belongs to such as these. Amen, I say to you, whoever does not accept the kingdom of God like a child will not enter it." Then he embraced them and blessed them, placing his hands on them.*

In another decade or two, you will be seeing increasingly larger families, and many of them home schoolers, appearing out of nowhere. You might wonder where they all have been hiding. This new generation will become the future leaders of our society, working to restore traditional Christian family values to our ailing country and beyond.

Many victims of our anti-child, anti-family culture have fallen prey to the notion that children are 'a burden.' Some still choose to have only one or two children in order to be socially acceptable and have dinner table talk on their business trips. Yet, an increasing number of couples simply choose to have no children at all. At least they are honest. They know they are not interested in raising children so they choose not to sacrifice innocent young minds to be preyed upon by the world in a pseudo-orphan life. To these couples, their career is their *life*, so they embrace it totally.

Even further, there are an increasing number of people who choose not to marry. *"Why be tied down?"* they think to themselves. For some, marriage is viewed as old-fashioned and a road block in front of the pursuit of their hopes and dreams of the glory of this world.

We now have abortions, pills, and other procedures to make parenting completely optional. Are we better off because of it? Back in the 1930's when some mainline Christian denominations declared artificial contraception as morally acceptable, the institution of marriage was forever changed. No longer was it a cherished mystery of the potential creation of a human life. The intimacy between a husband and wife was diminished to 'a good time' and the creating life part, well, that was completely left up to the couple.

An increasing number of Christian married couples are *completely* committed to raising their family as God-centered. This means they are open to life – namely, *children.* These families, though a small, yet extremely fast-growing minority, plan to bring back the sanctity of marriage and the traditional Judeo-Christian family.

Think about this for a moment. Ten children raised from a traditional Christian home become ready to start their own families. Many of these children will marry, have several more children, and raise them with similar values. Some of the children may become priests or ministers, preaching to families about

46

taking their role seriously by living the gospel message in home and outward. All the while, the childless couples and single individuals are dying out. The one or two children raised from the two-parent working environment have been left feeling that parenting is of little importance. If they have any children at all, it is likely they may carry on the unfortunate tradition of their own parents: lack of time in the home. Then, again, maybe they will be like you or me and decide "things are going to be different for *our* family!"

Concern for Overpopulation

There are communist governments that kill off their own nation, even to the extent of killing children in front of their own parents. Our country isn't *that* far off *yet*, but it *could* be in the near future if this culture of death we live in continues. It really *is* a culture of death. We work. We make money. We have fun. We die. Is that what you really want the little dash on your tombstone to mean? (you know, the one between your birth date and your death date.) The most rapidly-increasing portion of the population in some communist societies is the senior citizens. The false fear of over-population is why some nations set up anti-life laws. In the case of a one-child-per-family law, a nation could cut its population in half each generation. If it weren't for immigration, the United States would be experiencing a *declining* population. The myth of overpopulation has long been disproved. The unequal distribution of goods throughout the world continues to fool people. This world is much bigger than we think.

Did someone figure out the math in all this? The 'liberal agenda' as is often referred to, is putting itself out of business-or so it seems. Ah, but watch out! They are after *your* children in the public school system and through the media. Their largest resource of new followers is converts –few babes are born into their 'religion.' This is why it is so crucial that we raise our children our*selves* - so we are able to instill in them *our* faith and values. Deuteronomy 6:4-9 exhorts us emphatically to: *"Hear, O Israel! The LORD is our God, the LORD alone! Therefore, you shall love the LORD, your God, with all your heart, and with all*

47

your soul, and with all your strength. Take to heart these words which I enjoin on you today. Drill them into your children. Speak of them at home and abroad, whether you are busy or at rest. Bind them at your wrist as a sign and let them be as a pendant on your forehead. Write them on the doorposts of your houses and on your gates."

What does this scripture say to you? To me, it says that it takes a lot of *time* to correctly and thoroughly instill our values and beliefs into our little children's minds and hearts. By working outside the home, I fear that mothers have doomed themselves to failure. They may be the most well-intentioned, hardest working moms around, but they keep forgetting that they and their children are only *human beings*. We live in such a technologically-advanced society that sometimes we forget we can't just push a button and program the essential teachings into our children. To you mothers who dropped off your infants or young children that first day into the daycare, the child-care provider's home, or the preschool: How did you feel? Liberated? Think back. Remember. Your heart – how did your heart feel? Torn out of your soul! Yes! But you buried that hurt and told yourself to 'get a grip' because this is the 'real world'. Yes, it is. But remember, we as Christians are not *of this world.* We need to focus on the Lord's call for us.

Natural Mothering

Each and every mother is given a special gift of attachment to her baby. It is unnatural to go against this gift. God provided some of this attachment by way of breastfeeding hormones. I believe every mother should be encouraged to try to breastfeed while I understand that in some unfortunate cases this isn't possible. In our society, some women are enticed into bottle-feeding so they won't become 'inconvenienced' or so the baby won't become 'too attached' to their mommies. After all, they need to become 'independent' as soon as possible, right? How sad! We have much to learn from other cultures, such as tribal Africa, where the mother and baby are virtually inseparable for the first three years of life. Among the animal families, even the elephants can provide inspiration to us in their mothering techniques.

I've personally found that by continuing to breastfeed each child throughout his siblings' pregnancy (most of our children were 18 months apart in age) he was far less prone to jealousy of the new baby, since he could have 'the other side' during nursing sessions. I have experienced newborns in the home *without* the previous child still nursing, and found the jealousy to be a real challenge to the family.

Some families have turned back to the old 'family bed' approach, letting the child gradually learn independent sleeping as opposed to forcing it on them too soon. We have used this technique to a degree for our babies and it has allowed for more flexibility and quality sleep during their first year and beyond.

When I became pregnant with our first child, I was thrilled and wanted to be the 'perfect mother.' A new friend served as my mentor and invited me to La Leche League meetings so I could learn the whys and hows of breastfeeding. Sebrina turned out to be a seemingly healthy baby but very demanding at the breast. My mother teased that she didn't know what our daughter's face looked like until she was a year old since she nursed so often! Sebrina and I were very blessed to have been nursing during her baby and toddler years. In fact, I feel certain she would not have survived if it weren't for the small but essential nutrition she was getting from my milk during her serious illness which I will describe next.

Tough Times

When Sebrina was a toddler she became deathly ill and later required major surgery. Her long illness was a mystery to most doctors, until at last she was diagnosed with misplaced uretur tubes that needed to be re-implanted. This deformity had caused her urine to back-up into her kidneys from the time of her birth.

Evidently, the intensely frequent breastfeeding during her first year of life must have protected her from chronic illness, because it wasn't until after that first year that she began exhibiting symptoms. We had thought she was just 'advanced for her age' when her diapers remained dry at night from late infancy onward.

Shortly after her first birthday, she was struck with a deadly case of intestinal parasites, along with my husband and me, although the origin baffled the doctors. It was determined later that most people (including me who also tested positive but had no symptoms) with strong immune systems would not be affected by intestinal parasites. On the flip side, those with already weakened immune systems were at risk of a long battle to overcome such microorganisms. We knew why Dave was susceptible. He was plagued with a sleep disorder and, despite treatment, was more prone to illness at that time. He became extremely ill and lost quite a bit of weight over those next several weeks, though he had none to spare.

Sebrina's case went on for so many months she was finally referred to the most 'reputable' children's hospital in the country, which just happened to be in our own city of Indianapolis. I was extremely uneasy about the appointment, knowing that a little fifteen-month-old baby girl had died there recently. This tragedy was not caused from her *illness*, but, unthinkably, from an *overdose of potassium* incorrectly administered by a nurse. This little baby and her family had a special place in my heart. Recently I had donated my own breast milk to sustain her through a feeding tube over a period of months. The mother had previously weaned the child and was unable to produce milk when the doctors told her breast milk would be the only tolerable source of nutrition for her tiny daughter. Since I was still nursing Sebrina (about two years old) and her newborn brother, Nathan, at the time, I had plenty of milk to spare.

We found the doctors at the children's hospital to be callous and robotic. Any parents going through what we were at the time (or worse) would be in need of a compassionate doctor at this point. Being first-time parents, we were all the more worried and unsure of ourselves. These insensitive doctors used our inexperience to doubt our credibility concerning the severity of our daughter's lack of nutrition. We had watched her lose weight week after week for months but were repeatedly told she would 'outgrow it.' Being referred to the 'best pediatric gastroenterologist in the country' proved to be a cruel joke. My life became an endless stream of trips with Sebrina to the laboratory to drop off countless stool specimens that always had to be delivered within the hour. The medications used for treating Sebrina's current intestinal infection were brutal, to say the least, and have left her system vulnerable to severe cases of stomach or intestinal viruses ever since.

Down the road, an exceptionally intuitive, sympathetic pediatrician discovered that Sebrina suffered from chronic urinary tract infections. This possibility was never even tested for by the staff at the children's hospital. The new doctor quickly decided her case was unusually stubborn and recommended a urologist. The specialist treated her with two years of increasingly harsher antibiotics, yet there was no real cure in sight. Our trips to the lab over *these* next two years were intertwined with a parade of urine samples and a few stool samples now and again when her stools would look suspicious. Sebrina was now enduring cystoscopies (treatments where the doctor applies medication directly into the bladder.) After several of these 'sure to cure' procedures, this reputable urologist threw up his hands and offered no referral, hoping only that she might 'outgrow' this potentially life-threatening illness.

Due in part to her long battle with intestinal parasites, if a stomach virus took hold of Sebrina, it became life-threatening. I remember helplessly watching her vomit stomach acid every 15 minutes for hours on end, not even able to keep a single sliver of ice down. She was listlessly dehydrated and agitated, only consoled by my reading stories for hours until she would again drift off to a drugged sleep. It was clear in my mind that my full-time job had shifted from 'homemaker' to 'caretaker' and I couldn't have imagined coming even close to meeting Sebrina's unique health needs had I been employed outside the home. By the tender age of two, she had undergone a tonsillectomy, been hospitalized twice for severe stomach flu, and was now facing possible kidney damage with no cure in sight.

51

The doctor at the time tried to provide the best of care, including middle-of-the-night phone consultations on several occasions; but he refused to admit her into the hospital that winter for fear she would die from the dreaded RSV virus that was filling the hospital pediatric ward. He knew her system was extremely weak and vulnerable. He had given her a series of gamma-globulin shots to boost her immune system, not commonly prescribed by other pediatricians who were at a loss to help her.

Finally, as a last resort, she again had to return to the hospital for IV treatment. Her veins were (and still are) so tiny and easily collapsible that the IV machine would often ring out the dreaded 'beep,' meaning that her IV had once again stopped working. This meant a new IV would need to go into her tiny arm. For a two-year-old, this is a traumatic experience. For Sebrina, it was heart-wrenching. Nurse after nurse would try, without success, to administer the IV into her veins. Finally, without fail, an anesthesiologist had to be called in from the emergency room to insert the new IV.

Unfortunately, no matter how many times we tried to explain the difficulty of her IV dilemma to the nurses, every time it would again go out, the available nurse at the time would assure us "I'm very experienced at this," only to again begin the horrific and tortuous process that inevitably took two hours, several nurses, another anesthesiologist, and the result: many bruises and an extremely hysterical child and distraught parents.

When Sebrina turned three, we were led to an angelic, competent urologist who immediately diagnosed Sebrina's problem through more hospital tests. Once she was forced to urinate on a towel in front of several medical personnel in order that they may track her urine (which had been dyed) to see if it was heading for the kidneys. That test saved her life.

Finally we had our long-awaited-for diagnosis and a treatment to cure it. The surgery wouldn't be easy – her little insides would have to be rearranged so her urine would follow the correct path. Although the ideal for any surgery is to wait until the patient is 'stable,' this was not a possibility in Sebrina's case. We would just have to take the risk that her immune system may become further weakened by the surgery before she would someday become healthy. The day after surgery, Sebrina was attached to a multitude of tubes and monitoring machines. We prayed this would be her turn-around to good health. During those long eight days in the hospital, I never failed to keep our little nursing son, Nathan, at my side. I was thankful that he was still young enough to take along easily. The nurses sometimes worried about him catching germs, but they also realized with the full-time attention Sebrina required, my leaving Nathan behind would only add to my stress as well as the entire family's. Besides, Nathan's little chubby, smiling face was some of the best medicine for Sebrina at that time.

At one point, only a week after being discharged from her bladder surgery, Sebrina was again attacked by the dreaded stomach virus. She was so severely ill it was a miracle we didn't lose her. Nurses regularly underestimated our wisdom and ignored our pleas to keep her on liquids longer so as not to start the vomiting cycle all over again. They insisted we were inexperienced parents and that she needed to start eating again to "get her strength up." We knew that it took her several days on liquids in order to tolerate solid food after such an illness. In fact, we were regularly stocked with anti-nausea suppositories at home that, in most cases, would only be used as a last resort. In Sebrina's case, it eventually came to be that the suppositories would sedate her and keep her from vomiting, but she would be too weak to be interested in any nourishment so it defeated the purpose it was designed to accomplish.

As new parents, we were normally very camera-happy with Sebrina. But during these sad months, we refrained from taking pictures of our little toddler girl since her hair had become straw-like and her little body was so frail and weak. Many times during Sebrina's illness, the offer of my breast was the only thing her stomach tolerated that would calm her and give her at least a few drops of the nutrition her body starved for but otherwise could not tolerate.

By embracing God's plan for natural mothering, I was able to bear a very difficult situation by the knowledge that I was offering Sebrina everything I had as a mother. The fact that I was home full-time during those years enabled me to avoid further stress from my employer announcing, "If you can't return to work soon I'm afraid we're going to have to let you go." By the same token, had Sebrina been in a daycare situation, it is unlikely that I would have been tuned-in enough to recognize her obscure health problem; but as it was I was available to persist from doctor to doctor until I found a solution. It can't be forgotten that the prayers and support of our brothers and sisters in Christ were a godsend throughout Sebrina's ordeal.

Although our other children have been relatively healthy overall, some have undergone surgeries for various problems. We've been through tonsillectomies, ear tubes, an appendectomy, ingrown toenails, severe plantar warts, a couple of broken bones, and even RSV (a severe respiratory virus known to be fatal to infants.) For the RSV I stayed in an oxygen tent for three days with Victor, our ninth child, age six weeks at the time. I was able to be fully present each time my family needed me.

We have had other trying situations, including my husband's neck surgery, which required a six-week recovery, and our oldest son who had severe food allergies, chronic diarrhea and subsequent behavior problems that took another couple of years of my detective work and perseverance to remedy. My husband, Dave, has suffered from a sleep disorder and Obsessive-Compulsive Disorder our whole married life. Some treatments have helped and very recently just about cured his symptoms. But all the while, through no fault of his own, Dave was unable to emotionally connect to our family nearly as well as he wanted to. This caused considerable friction between the two of us and the family as a whole many times and may have contributed to our oldest child's current taste of rebellion. Our daughter, Sebrina, actually helped support me in writing this book. Sadly, she's taken a different road just recently, and some of yours may do the same. But we pray it's temporary – and there are some excellent books for Parents of Prodigals out there if you need one. I highly recommend, "*The Hope of a Homecoming,*" *Entrusting Your Prodigal to a Sovereign God,* by Brendan O'Rourke, Ph.D. and DeEtte Sauer.

54

This doesn't mean that staying home and doing your best doesn't work. It means our kids have free will. They make wrong choices. And it means we make mistakes that they may hold against us. But it's all a part of life. None of us have perfect families. We all will have our struggles – some bigger than others – and if Mommies stay home through the brunt of child-rearing it will certainly serve as an anchor that is steadying the ups and downs of our family life. Sometimes it's the Mommy herself who struggles with mental, emotional or physical illness. In this case she needs all the support she can get – but advising her to seek a career during this time could further detriment the family stability that is so desperately needed during our trying times. I believe competent Christian counseling is essential to get through these rough spots in any family. It certainly has helped us through many crises.

It works both ways. Particularly with the flexibility provided by home schooling, my family was able to be there for me when I approached and recovered from my two carpal tunnel hand surgeries, greatly limiting my hand use for several months, as well as three C-section deliveries. In fact, grandparents pitched in quite a bit, since they weren't already burned out by full-time childcare responsibilities.

Life is already full of challenges. It's probably enough of a trial just for a career Mom to get a half-day off work for her child's doctor appointment. When the child is too sick for daycare, and Grandma is too feeble to be exposed, Mom or Dad will again need to stay home. Maybe you are experiencing health problems in your own family. Some of you may have a mentally or physically handicapped child. Some of you may have lost a home to a tornado or a fire. God allows suffering to different degrees for different people, each according to His plan for their life. If our primary job is to meet the needs of our family, then we can be ready and able to do that job during tough times when our family needs us the most. No one intentionally brings suffering upon their own family. But by rejecting God's ultimate plan for our motherhood, we are unknowingly inviting a road-of-life race into our home in which the winner has been rigged – the culture of death, otherwise known as Satan. He has already claimed the victory *if* we submit to the ways of the world. We don't have to look too far to see the broken-family results of the victories of the Devil.

Okay, So What About *Me*?

Maybe you are feeling a bit deflated at this point. Do you feel as if I'm saying to you that your only job is to be a mother? Am I telling you to just cash in all your talents, intellect, and personality to merely become a perpetual need-filler? No, I wouldn't say that at all.

In fact, as a Christian, I would like to call attention to the greatest mother of all. *Mary, the mother of Jesus,* surrendered her entire future for the sake of the salvation of mankind. Without delving into heavy theology, let me simply say that she considered it a great honor and privilege to accept her role as mother to the Son of God. Many look to her as an example of holy motherhood. Nowhere in the Bible does it state that Mary felt it was a burden to be a mother. Her burden was in the *suffering* of her Son. She expressed *joy* in the motherhood experience. *And Mary said:*

"My soul proclaims the greatness of the Lord;
    my spirit rejoices in God my savior.
For he has looked upon his handmaid's lowliness;
    behold, from now on will all ages call me blessed.
The Mighty One has done great things for me,
    and holy is his name. (Luke 1:46-49)

This world cannot be our measure of what is valuable. The Lord created male and female to have separate and distinct roles in the family. If we choose to gain glory for ourselves instead of for the Lord, then our families will crumble. There is much room in our home for our talents, creativity and abilities. I find it surprising that many women, who seem confident in the workplace, express inadequacy within the context of their role as mother. They often say, "I don't have the patience to stay home all day," or, "I just don't think I would be a good teacher for my children." Ironically, some of these mothers *are* teachers – of someone *else's* children, without the advantage of sharing their students' genes or knowing their strengths and weaknesses. It's almost like a nurse saying she fears she cannot treat her child's scraped knee. If God blessed us with children then He automatically offers us sufficient grace and strength to raise them up if we would only ask for help. I think our commitment of time is much more important than our 'ability' or lack thereof. Many times ability comes with experience.

Chapter 6   So, How Do You 'Do it'?

This question is often asked of me, as if wondering how I've mastered a triple back-flip off the high-dive. I think parenthood is a *process*. The commitment itself is greater than the actual tasks involved. By true definition, *we* can't accomplish this feat on our own; we must draw on the strength of the Lord and His infinite wisdom. *"For human beings it is impossible, but not for God. All things are possible for God." Mark 10:27*

Let the Media Serve Your Family -- (Not the Other Way Around)

When we first married we read parenting books and discussed at length how we would raise our children; (we had to hurry since I became pregnant on our honeymoon!) The very first thing we did was get rid of our TVs. It was such a huge part of our growing-up years; we felt the 'boob tube' would overcome our attempts to have a Christ-centered home. After seven years, we did slowly introduce the 'silly box' into the family environment with very tight restrictions. Even to this day, if I hear one of our children turn on the TV, I know for a fact they must be inserting their science lab video, otherwise it probably is our toddler getting into mischief. They simply do not touch it unless they have permission to do so.

Recently, we acquired a satellite dish that provides us with wholesome Christian programming. *Familyland TV* is our favorite network. (See the resource list at the end of this book for details.) One day the satellite system went down and our oldest daughter decided to tune into an old favorite: *20/20*. The commercials were quite offensive to her after being away from 'real TV' for so long.

59

The media uses dysfunctional families to promote convenience items. Example: disrespectful children speaking unkindly are given granola bars to 'shut them up'. The advertisement stated 'Chewy stops the chatter.' One ad promotes a three-way phone line splitter to facilitate non-cooperation among family members. That way no one needs to compromise or spend time together – each family member can then retreat to his own room to indulge in his own private activity. We can't let the media dictate how our families will be. Keep in mind these are just the *commercials* and we all know the programs are far worse examples of wholesome family life.

Our children associate TV with family time, when we all snuggle on the couch*es (remember we're a big family!)* together with our bowls of popcorn and watch a great family movie. In fact, several times when I've offered a thirty-minute video or children's program to the kids, they respond with "Sorry, Mom, but we're busy building or playing house, etc." Unless we're watching a special movie (during which we're interacting with one another about what's happening,) we've found that an hour a day, even of the best of Christian TV or video entertainment is the limit for our children. Beyond that, the kids become irritable, glossy-eyed and may even beg for another show in a monotonic whine, yet they're really saying, "Turn this thing off! – I'm buzzed!"

The fact is that when our children have been allowed to be creative, they will often choose to keep busy with their own little minds, hands, and bodies over passive entertainment. This is a credit to their creator, God, to their potential for learning. We, as parents, merely must try to avoid stunting that creative potential.

It's the same with our computer. We have a filter, which is essential; however, none of our children go on the computer without permission unless it's for typing their school papers. They associate the computer with education. "Mom, will you help me search the web for this report?" "Can I practice my computer flash cards?" Or wholesome fun, "Can I make a chess move with Uncle Harvey this morning?"

We have also tried to be extremely careful about what kind of music we listen to. When children are raised with Christian, classical and family-friendly music around them, secular music will *disturb* them rather than tempt them. When it's time to clean house, we crank up the praise and worship music, or a soundtrack from a great classic musical. It focuses our minds on 'things from above' rather than dragging us down in an already sin-laden world. In our vehicles, it's the same. Why tune into questionable radio stations when today there's so much variety offered in the Christian realm? All media affects our thoughts, (whether subconscious or conscious) which in turn affects our actions and what comes out of our mouths. We try to recite this together frequently from a big poster in our eating area: **WHATEVER**...
"Finally,... whatever is true, whatever is honorable, whatever is just, whatever is pure, whatever is lovely, whatever is gracious, if there is any excellence and if there is anything worthy of praise, think about these things" Phillipians 4:8.

Eating the World One Bite at a Time

You may say our children sound too sheltered. If children are exposed to the entire 'real world' too quickly, it creates a stimulation overload. First, they need to be given controlled opportunities to formulate their values. If we want a safe society, all children must learn right from wrong. I guarantee they won't learn it on the school playground or even on the church soccer team. The adults may do their best to teach the rules, but the surrounding peers far outnumber the adults! Many of their peers, I might add, come from broken homes with little or no intact value system.

When children are put into bite-size situations in which they can act upon their family's values, they will then become more confident and better able to handle the next situation that comes their way. However, when drowned out too heavily by the weight of this world's influences, they will feel like the tiniest whos in Whoville shouting, (and maybe in vain) "We're here! We're here! We're here!"

Three of our pre-teen and teenage children played on the same soccer team where a fellow player was being mocked and teased by the rest of the team. The perpetrator was actually an older *sibling* of the victim! This went on for several days and one day our children were approached and pressured to join in. They stood strong and rebuked the child, asking why he would treat his sister in this way. Our children believe in defending other kids who are ostracized by the 'in-group.' There's a fine line between self-righteousness, and charity, but with our help and much prayer, our children try to walk that line. They've lost some friendships because of their refusal to laugh along or participate in ungodly behavior. But they have *each other*! They find such encouragement and reassurance within the family. They realize it's not possible to agree with everyone or be liked by everyone in this world (or even in their family.) They must stand for what is right, be forgiving, charitable, and keep their humility in check. This is a constant process for all of us.

So Hard to Find Good Help These Days

In any work environment, individuals must learn to submit to authority while maintaining their ability to think for themselves. There have been some ideal work opportunities we've encouraged for our kids. Three of our children, starting at ages eleven, and up to age fifteen, were soccer referees for several seasons. This has taught them how to interact with other adults, be a role model for other children, and become responsible for their paperwork and equipment.

Our oldest daughter wanted to work for a specific restaurant chain and applied to it exclusively because of its Christian business ethics. They told her, "Sorry, honey, we don't hire anyone under the age of sixteen." Not easily discouraged, she stated, simply, "Oh, that's okay, I'll be *fourteen* (legal working age in Georgia) next month!" After persevering with her portfolio of recommendation letters from satisfied babysitting clients and attending two interviews, she landed herself a job. As a result of working, she was able to save for and pay cash for her own car at age 16. This was good news because she didn't want to drive our big van or station wagon and she was soon to be attending a local college. Heaven knows I had enough running to do without having to drop a college kid off at class too! The confidence needed in order to make her first major decisions had been instilled all along by her time-generous family and faith life.

Practice Makes Perfect

Within the context of the home school environment we're able to read and discuss books on character and faith. We have many opportunities *among ourselves* to learn forgiveness! As much as we'd like to at times, it's not possible to storm out of the house for the rest of the day and ignore each other, which happens in families when each person goes their separate way every morning. We are forced to get along and communicate. We clean and cook together. We study and pray together. We laugh and cry together. We even have a family mission statement in the form of a song, *"Communicate, cooperate and love one another. Pray together; play together each and every day. Let's plan for our future and reach out to those in need. Pray together; play together each and every day."* After our bedtime prayers we sing this song twice to the tune of "Ode to Joy" while giving each other backrubs. (Alright, it may sound corny – but it's fun-loving and it helps.)

The Velveteen Rabbit Became REAL

Do we love our children enough to make them become 'real' as the velveteen rabbit in the classic children's story? Do you say this isn't the 'real world?' In the 'real world' the best business leaders are those who can mediate and resolve conflict. If they grew up with conflict avoidance, they will not be trained to handle such challenges in the workplace. In the 'real world,' people are all ages and backgrounds. In the public and private school systems, children are surrounded all day by people of the same age (their own.)

At home, we are all ages, and have the freedom to invite those of different nationalities and backgrounds into our home to learn about the world around us. Although the media won't admit it, the real world is full of exclusive groups. My husband once attended a church with a friend in which the entire congregation was made up of either current or former electrical engineers! After being raised in naturally racially balanced neighborhoods, my husband and I were shocked to find we had once moved into an all-white residential area. This was quite contrary to our way of thinking and we had to go out of our way to show our children the 'real world.' In the 'real world' we must be able to think for ourselves and make many decisions each day, either at home or in the workplace. In a daycare or public school environment most decisions are made for our children. Children are led along in a herd-style from one activity to the next. But at home we can empower our children with the opportunity to learn smart and effective decision-making skills.

In the 'real world' if we get a speeding ticket, we must pay the fine. If we want to buy something, we must save our money or pay interest on a loan. Yet how many worn-out working parents indulge their children by bailing them out of consequences or rewarding them for acceptable, yet not exceptional, behavior? In the 'real world' we do not get a cookie if we show up to work on time. Yet, so many rushed parents reward their children if they promise 'not to make a scene.' No, ladies, we do not want the 'real world' by its common definition. In fact the 'real world' is *our family* – we are the foundation of society, the 'church in miniature.' What is *real within our homes* becomes *real within society.* Let's keep that in mind as we reflect on how each one of us can do our part to fulfill our true vocation of motherhood.

Epilogue

One week old – newborn bliss

She heard that familiar sucking sound coming from the crib just a few feet away from the bed. *Funny how I always wake up at the same time he does*, Nancy thought, walking over to pick up her nursing newborn. It was his third nursing session that night, but she didn't mind. She tucked baby Matthew between herself and her husband, Tom, and offered him the breast. He sucked eagerly as she tenderly gazed at his tiny features by the hazy glow of the night light. She felt such satisfaction, knowing that she could provide for so many of her baby's needs just by breastfeeding, and pondered what an awesome plan the Lord had for mothers and babies to bond from the very start.

Five weeks old – hurry-up bonding

All those parenting books never did relay the reality of this immense love I feel for our child, she thought, while drying off little Matthew from his morning bath. Knowing this would be the last week of maternity leave, Nancy was relishing every moment of time with her infant son. There were so many tasks to be done around the house and errands to be run, but that would all have to wait. This was her bonding time with Matthew. He looked up at her, gazing into her eyes with such trust and complete dependence.

A few days later – time running out

The breast pump was malfunctioning again, as Nancy attempted to begin the process of pumping and storing her milk in preparation for returning to work. "This just doesn't feel natural; I feel like a *cow!*" she said to her husband after another pumping session. *Maybe I should just put him on formula and make life easy on myself. I think this nursing thing is overrated anyway*, she told herself, trying to ignore the inner pangs of dread that had

67

enveloped her as the last day before returning to work approached nearer.

Six weeks old – back to the 'real world'

She jumped out of bed to the noise of the blaring alarm clock, which also woke Matthew. He had been fussy the past couple of nights so Nancy was exhausted. *What a way to start back to work*, she thought, wondering if Matthew was getting colicky from the new formula. There was no time to waste, so Matthew was dressed as quickly as possible and before long Mother and child were packed up and backing down the driveway for their first day in the 'real world.'

We No Best Day Care Center had seemed really nice during the open house tour. Everything had been so clean and organized, and the workers were very caring and compassionate. Today when walking in the door, however, all Nancy could hear were babies crying, toddlers screaming, and rushed mothers dashing out to the parking lot empty-armed. After finding the newborn room, Nancy was told to go ahead and put Matthew in baby swing number six. "That way I'll remember which one he is" said the friendly worker. "Now don't you worry a bit – just go on and have yourself a great day!" assured the staff member.

By lunch time the stress became unbearable. Nancy *really* needed to see her baby. But there was so much work to do, and *We No Best* Day Care Center was too far a drive to make a round-trip for a thirty-minute lunch break. *I can call and check on him*, she thought.

She was put on hold for five minutes when finally a woman came to the phone announcing, "Your *daughter* is just fine, "Ma'am". She slept and ate real good and messed up plenty of diapers for us." Nancy was **mortified**! "Excuse me, did you say *daughter*?! I have a *son – Matthew Miller!*" "Er um, sorry about the little mix-up there – no problem, I'll run and check on the little feller," said the embarrassed employee.

Picking him up after work, Nancy couldn't help but notice the flat spot on the back of Matthew's head. "Did he sleep a lot today?" She asked a staff member. "Well, *yea*, those newborns sleep all the time, Ma'am, and we don't like them to get germs or nothin' so we just try to keep them clean and safe in their cribs as much as possible." "I see," answered Nancy, her heart sinking. Matthew was in a deep sleep all the way home, seemingly shutting out the negative environment he had sensed all day. Nancy remembered reading about how newborns will sleep more to shut out stress or stimuli they can't handle any other way. *Surely he will be off his schedule, now*, she thought, as she buckled him into his carseat.

In the middle of the night, Matthew screamed and cried for hours. He didn't have a fever. He was not calmed by anything Nancy or her husband tried to do to console him. He even refused the breast, offered as a last resort, although emptied of milk now since it had been several days since he last nursed.

Three months old – looking for love

Nancy had been looking forward to this all week. Mrs. Babylove, a customer from the office with three young children, had invited her for lunch on Saturday. The personable young woman mentioned that she had a spot for a newborn at her in-home daycare. *This would be so much better for Matthew*, thought Nancy. *The extra money spent would be worth the peace of mind in knowing our baby could be in a home environment.*

After only two weeks in his new home-based daycare environment, Matthew was thriving. He was sleeping better during the night at home; in fact, he was developing quickly - surely a result of his new stable surroundings. "Oh, I wish you could have seen him roll over today!" Mrs. Babylove, exclaimed, "his little face just lit up and he smiled the biggest grin! The kids were his personal cheerleaders!"

Little Matthew often reached for the arms of Mrs. Babylove upon being dropped off in the morning, and cried regularly when being picked up at dinner time. After one particularly rough pick-up experience, Nancy thought, *it's almost like Susan's family is more significant to Matthew than his Daddy or me. Maybe he needs to be with **real** family.*

Six months old – grandparents to the rescue

Grandma and Grandpa were looking forward to this new adventure of keeping up with their active little grandson, Matthew. After all, they had had plenty of practice now on weekends when Nancy and Tom needed an evening out. What could be more satisfying than knowing they will be contributing to their young grandson's college education fund by allowing his mother to earn and save the salary for which she was educated?

Eighteen months old – need a nanny

Matthew had become increasingly prone to tantrums. Nancy and Tom were getting concerned about Tom's parents' health. It was obvious that they couldn't keep up with Matthew, and the energetic toddler was very frustrated at being cooped up inside their home all day. The evenings were too hectic to make time for friendships between toddlers, and preschool was a long way off.

Tom suggested hiring a local nanny with whom a coworker was pleased before being transferred out of state. Mrs. Stickler came over the next day to meet Matthew. After a few days of interviews, and nanny-meets-youngster experiences, Nancy decided she'd best get back to work and give this a fair try. The nanny seemed to meet all of Matthew's physical needs, but, unlike the in-home care provider, she didn't connect emotionally to Matthew. Mrs. Stickler also maintained such a rigid schedule for Matthew, there was no consideration for his moods or 'off days.' After a few weeks, the strain began to build, and Tom read an article on the internet urging parents with nannies to install video and audio recording equipment to protect their children in case of abuse. Tom had already mentioned to Nancy his feeling that their privacy was invaded and they both felt the pressure to keep the place extra tidy since they knew Mrs. Stickler would be coming each day. The whole idea just wore thin and Nancy and Tom jointly decided to dismiss the nanny.

Nineteen months old – Mr. Mom on the scene

Nancy had done so well with her career that her recent sizeable promotion actually put her salary higher than Tom's. Tom wasn't at all threatened by this. In fact, he was extremely proud of his wife and, after considering all the childcare turmoil they had been through, felt that the loving thing to do at this point would be to become a full-time Dad. It only made sense that the highest earner should be the primary breadwinner. Spending one-on-one time with his little son this final year before registering him in preschool would be a small sacrifice in light of all the joys that would surely accompany his decision. He sort of mused at the thought of being called 'Mr. Mom.'

Two years old – reality sets in

Tom's enthusiasm waned thinner and thinner as the months went on. He really missed the recognition and adult conversation of his workplace. Nancy had noticed on several occasions upon coming home from work that Tom would be "scanning the news" on the computer, or repairing something around the house while Matthew was getting into some serious mischief! "He was just in here a *second* ago!" chided Tom, defending himself again. "How is a parent supposed to get anything done with a two-year-old in the house?" Tom's inability to focus on more than one thing at a time led to many near-disasters for Matthew. A couple of times the toddler nearly choked and once almost succeeded in sticking a fork into the electrical outlet. Tom learned to use the child carrier or try to plan his chores during Matthew's nap and TV time, but it often became very frustrating. It was obvious Tom was feeling defeated and longing for the career he once enjoyed.

Nancy was nervous as she approached her boss's office. "It's just not working out at home, Mr. Shale. We've tried every childcare arrangement we could think of and, based on his behavior, little Matthew just isn't fairing well. Would you consider allowing me to do some computer work at home? I could certainly keep up with the load if I had the peace-of-mind in knowing my little son was playing happily at my feet."

"Well," responded Mr. Shale, looking intrigued, "I definitely think it's worth a try. You have been a prized engineer for us and we do have some web design programs that could be implemented just as easily from your home computer. Just remember, our agency does require prompt delivery of our design packages, so let's just give this a month's trial and hope for the best!" Nancy was elated and so relieved. She beamed a huge smile and thanked Mr. Shale as she shook his hand with extra firmness.

That evening, Nancy shared the news with Tom over dinner out while Matthew stayed with a sitter. The couple knew this was surely the answer to their parenting woes. By the following month, Tom was getting settled in with a prominent company while Nancy was finding out for the first time what it was like to stay home.

Superwoman comes home
Two weeks into the new routine

Nancy had lofty ideals of surpassing the expectations of her boss. She had a good sense for Matthew's safety hazards and was very pleased to get him into a rigid routine that she could work around. Tom and Nancy invested in some excellent cable programming complete with several networks chock full of children's shows. Matthew was well-stocked with countless battery-operated toys and enticing snack foods to keep him from getting underfoot while Nancy worked on the computer and made business calls. It became necessary to hire a teenager for a few hours each day in order for Nancy to attend required weekly meetings at the office or run important business errands. She knew she had to appear professional, and taking a two-year-old along to business meetings or even to the local office supply store surely didn't seem appropriate from that standpoint.

It was surprising, too, at how many business expenses were accumulating. In addition, neither Tom nor Nancy had anticipated all the extra *things* that would be 'needed' in order to keep Matthew occupied and out of trouble. To their shock, Matthew often threw his expensive toys around and refused to watch TV! He was often whining about wanting Mommy to read or color with him. Every time Nancy got on the phone or the computer Matthew took full advantage and became destructive. He acted just plain spoiled. Nancy finally admitted to herself, *This just isn't going to work.*

Two years, three months old – sinking fast

Nancy was at the end of her rope. Tom was at a loss of what to do for her. Mr. Shale had discussed with Nancy that she needed to return to the office by the following week in order to keep her position since she had fallen short of meeting the design deadline. Nancy felt like a failure. She was binge eating, had gained fifteen pounds in just two weeks, and the house was a *pit*! Finally, Tom urged Nancy to see a counselor whom a friend at work suggested to be very helpful.

Two days later – So help me, God!

After only one session, the Christian counselor brought to surface the fact that Nancy was a fallen-away Christian. She had always been a believer, but it simply wasn't practical to try to balance a career, parenting, *and* church. There was just only so much a person could do. So, in Nancy's heart, she had never actually fallen away from her *faith*. It was still there, but it was malnourished and weak. It had been years since she'd read the Bible. She had to admit to herself that 'life in the fast lane' did not allow time for much prayer or meditation. Tom was also a believer, but it wasn't something the two talked about much. It was the basis for their faithful marriage and they were both honest, hard-working people. After all, that's what faith is all about, right? The Christian counselor exhorted Nancy to study several scriptures about the role and the duties of a Christian wife and mother. The counselor firmly, yet compassionately, pointed out that Nancy's circumstances and depression all stemmed from the fact that she had turned her back on God's plan for her vocation as a mother. The counselor suggested a brand new book entitled, *Mommy, Come Home*, for Nancy to read. It was a compelling, yet short book that tugged at Nancy's heart with lots of scripture-based practical ideas on how to embrace the role of full-time mother.

Within just a few weeks, Tom and Nancy made an offer on a smaller home, traded their new car in for a used one, and sold many of the unused fancy toys that never interested Matthew. They simplified their family life in a very real way. Matthew, although quite confused and spoiled by so many big changes in his short little life, was still pliable. Tom and Nancy had read that if they were consistent and dedicated, they could establish a new code of discipline and routine that Matthew could adjust to in just a few months' time.

74

Three years old – Mommy came home!

Tom walked through the door to the aroma of home-made lasagna, fresh baked bread, and his favorite dessert. Matthew came running to his Daddy with open arms and a messy 'junior-baker' smile. "I helped make dinner, Daddy!" Matthew proudly announced. "Look what me and Mommy made with playdough today!" he shouted, as he skipped through the house. "Now hold on for just a second while I kiss the woman I love," said Tom, as he grabbed Nancy around the waist and kissed her behind the neck in the kitchen. Nancy told Tom the great news about her doctor appointment, "Its official. We're due in May." "Matthew, you're going to be a big brother!" proclaimed Tom, scooping up Matthew to be included in a family huddle.

Later that evening, after Matthew was asleep, Tom and Nancy discussed the uneasiness they felt about placing Matthew into preschool the following year. They knew that Matthew would not get to bond with his new baby sibling as much if he were gone for a half-day every day. They had remembered reading about home-schooling in a couple of magazines, and hearing it mentioned on Christian radio. The book, *Mommy, Come Home* had also addressed the issue. They decided to pray about it and get some more details. Life for their family had so much more freedom, peace, and unity ever since *Mommy came home.*

Go with God, sister Moms

Let us endeavor to prepare our children for this world and the next. Together let's choose to raise godly children of upright moral character. As we mothers make the sacrifice, we will reap the reward of knowing our children *can* make a difference in this world – with eternal implications. Mommies, *please come home.*

Mary's Call: Our heavenly mother, Mary, answered her call to motherhood with great joy. Her obedience and humility is a guide for all Moms today. *"Behold, you will conceive in your womb and bear a son, and you shall name him Jesus. He will be great and will be called Son of the Most High, and the Lord God will give him the throne of David his father, and he will rule over the house of Jacob forever, and of his kingdom there will be no end."* But

Mary said to the angel, "How can this be, since I have no relations with a man?" And the angel said to her in reply, "The holy Spirit will come upon you, and the power of the Most High will overshadow you. Therefore the child to be born will be called holy, the Son of God, Luke 1:31-35

My Call: The Lord spoke to me and said, "*Sandy, you shall write a book and give it the name "Mommy, Come Home, begging mothers to stay home with their children.*" I answered the Lord, "*How can this be since I am not a professional author?*" The Lord answered me: "*The Holy Spirit will come upon you and you will not sleep for several days and nights. I will give you the energy needed to fulfill your motherly duties during the day, and at night while your children sleep my Spirit will guide your fingers at the computer keyboard in order that you create a compelling plea that will reach out and tug at every mother's heart, thus creating a new generation of Mothers fulfilling the will of God.*"

Your Call: *The Lord is speaking to you now, mom. Do you hear Him?*

"*Oh, that today you would hear his voice:*
    'Harden not your hearts as at the rebellion.'" (Hebrews 3:15)
"Yes, Lord, you know that I love you"

> *He then said to him a second time, "Simon, son of John, do you love me?" He said to him, "Yes, Lord, you know that I love you." He said to him, "Tend my sheep." (John 21:16)*

"But Lord," you answer, "How will I tell my boss and my family? What will my friends think? I'm not sure I can handle all that goes with full-time mothering"...

"There is no fear in love, but perfect love drives out fear because fear has to do with punishment, and so one who fears is not yet perfect in love." (1 John 4:18)

"But, Lord, I had plans"....

76

"For I know well the plans I have in mind for you, says the LORD, plans for your welfare, not for woe! plans to give you a future full of hope. When you call me, when you go to pray to me, I will listen to you. When you look for me, you will find me. Yes, when you seek me with all your heart, you will find me with you, says the LORD, and I will change your lot; I will gather you together from all the nations and all the places to which I have banished you, says the LORD, and bring you back to the place from which I have exiled you". (Jeremiah 29:11-15)

"I've made some mistakes – our home isn't what it should be". . .

"Finally, . . . rejoice. Mend your ways, encourage one another, agree with one another, live in peace, and the God of love and peace will be with you." (2nd Cor 13:11)

"I'm scared, and I feel so guilty – I wish I would have stayed home from the start."

> *"Be brave, my daughter. May the Lord of heaven grant you joy in place of your grief. Courage, my daughter.". . . (Tobit 7:17)*

"I feel confused and anxious. . . What if I lose my friends?"

Through your precepts I gain insight;
  therefore I hate all false ways. (Psalm 119:104)

> "Okay, Lord, I humbly accept your call to my vocation as a mother."

. . . "Well done, my good and faithful servant. Since you were faithful in small matters, I will give you great responsibilities. Come, share your master's joy." (Matthew 25:21)

77

Notes and references:

La Leche League offers breastfeeding support and an excellent cookbook, "Whole Foods for the Whole Family" that utilizes typical ingredients on hand for everyday practical cooking. Never be a slave to a recipe again! Personal note: I did not find their approach to discipline to be helpful beyond the age of 15 months – I prefer Dr. Dobson's approach (see Focus on the Family below) *www.lalecheleague.org*

Couple to Couple League teaches the art of Natural Family Planning and offers much help and support for your marriage and family living. *www.ccli.org*

Focus on the Family offers almost unlimited resources on any matter of Christian family life. *www.parenting.family.org*

Familyland TV network offers wholesome TV programming, marriage and family retreats, as well as resources to strengthen your family life. *www.familyland.tv*.

Home School Legal Defense Association offers legal counsel and support for home schooling families. *www.hslda.org*

Acknowledgements:

Chief Editors: Sebrina Gillmore and Linda Bass

Assistant editors: David, Nathan, Vinny, and Cassie Gillmore, Laurie Roberts

Inspiration provided by: The Holy Spirit, the Blessed Mother Mary, David, Sebrina, Nathan, Vinny, Cassie, Roch, Robby, Ben, Tina, Victor and Gabriel Gillmore, Bob and Madeline Gillmore, Esther Doyle *(MY MOM)*, Laurie Roberts and Linda Bass (my sisters), and my many stay-at-home Mom friends of whom I've been so privileged to know and love.

Author's Note: I would like to thank my large, noisy, entertaining family for their loving support and encouragement and for all the sacrifices they made during the long months it took me to write and edit this book. (Naturally most of it was written while they were *ASLEEP* in the middle of the night!)

About the Author: Sandra Gillmore, home-schooling mother of ten, resides in Warner Robins, Georgia with her husband, David, electrical engineer in civil service. In addition to full-time mothering, Sandy enjoys singing for church, baking, and reaching out to other moms to give and receive blessings and encouragement.

Printed in the United States
19988LVS00007B/646-747